EAST SUS
WALKS

EXPLORING
1066 country

Sandy Hernu

S.B. Publications

CONTENTS

Front Cover: *Herstmonceux Castle*
Back Cover: *Fishing boats, near Norman's Bay*
Title Page: *Camber Castle*

THE SUSSEX COAST 1066

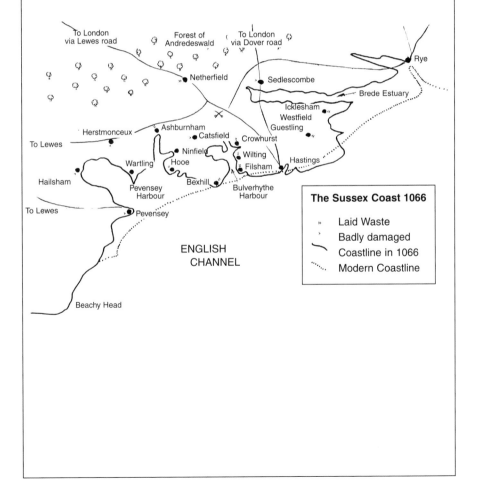

To London via Lewes road

Forest of Andredeswald

To London via Dover road

Rye

Netherfield

Sedlescombe

Brede Estuary

Icklesham
Westfield
Guestling

Herstmonceux

Ashburnham

Catsfield

Crowhurst

To Lewes

Ninfield

Wilting

Hastings

Wartling

Hooe

Filsham

Hailsham

Bexhill

Bulverhythe Harbour

Pevensey Harbour

To Lewes

Pevensey

ENGLISH CHANNEL

The Sussex Coast 1066

»   Laid Waste

›   Badly damaged

⌒   Coastline in 1066

······   Modern Coastline

Beachy Head

INTRODUCTION

Oh glorious Sussex, whose length and breadth of downland cossets valleys, villages and a network of footpaths, turning this hilly part of Southern England into a walker's paradise. But what of the countryside to the east? The Downs finish at the coastal cliffs of Beachy Head and the Sussex/Kent border lies on the other side of Rye, some thirty odd miles away. It appears that a great deal less is known (or written) about walking in this captivating area, stretching northwards beyond Bodiam Castle and having a charm, a beauty and a history all of its own.

The third book in the 'East Sussex Walks' series concentrates on this particular region, where the hills and meadows jostle side by side with castles and follies, capturing a delicious sense of a bygone era. Hopefully, it will entice the visitor, rambler or family to explore the domain made famous by William the Conqueror, when he and his vast retinue of soldiers fought and won the Battle of Hastings in 1066.

I always think of 1066 Country as being the gateway to Old England. The pageant of history from the time of the Norman Conquest is somehow easy to re-create in the imagination. So as we walk in the footsteps of Kings and Conquerors or wander across reclaimed land, where sheep have replaced ships, reflect for a moment or two on the turbulent past, which altered the course of our history and took place in this corner of Sussex.

The map shown gives an indication of the coastline both at that time and the present day; it has changed considerably. When the Conqueror landed at Pevensey, the Roman castle of Anderida stood neglected on a promontory. The invading Normans lost no time in rebuilding those castle walls, thus making a stronghold to guard the mouth of the estuary that swept back to Hailsham. Today the marshes that remain are flat and secretive; a delight to the birdwatcher, for all manner of wildlife live in the ditches and dykes. Part of the trail from Herstmonceux Castle to Wartling follows the old coastline and from there it is easy to envisage the once large and shallow harbour.

On the eastern edge of that same harbour stands Bexhill. A fairly large seaside resort now, but at the time of the invasion, it was merely a few houses, farm buildings and a wooden church, clustered on a low lying hill.

Attractive parts of the old village still remain and the church (no longer wooden) has some fine examples of Norman architecture.

At West Hill in Hastings, the Conqueror's favourite castle sits high on a rocky ridge above the quaint and narrow streets of Old Town, filled with an unending variety of intriguing shops. Opposite, the steep Cliff Railway ascends East Hill to Hastings Country Park, where the extensive cliff top walking offers some of the loveliest scenery in England.

Having passed Icklesham, the handsome church here is supposed to be the first the Normans built, the 1066 coastline drops back to form the narrow channel of the Brede estuary. This was extensively used by barges for the transportation of iron to Rye when Sedlescombe lay at the heart of the Wealden ironworks during the 16th and 17th centuries. In the 12th century, the ancient town of Rye was almost a hamlet compared to its neighbour, Winchelsea, whose fortunes changed after erosion caused the sea to recede, leaving Rye as the main port. Now it is a tourist's delight, with winding cobbled streets, potteries and a rich history.

Nudging inland towards Sedlescombe and Northiam, the countryside becomes hilly, wooded and unbelievably pretty, the properties being of the Kentish style, whitewashed and heavily timbered. Many of these inland villages have far-reaching views to the sea, a reminder that a number of them were deeply involved with the smuggling fraternity.

A book of 1066 walks would not be complete without visiting Battle and Battle Abbey, where the high altar of the church marks the spot where Harold fell. The trail meanders via the slopes and meadows that surround the Abbey and through the landscape where so much bloodshed took place.

I have alluded to just a few of the gems harboured in the 1066 countryside; there are plenty more to see on any one of the circular walks that travel through this gentle and golden terrain. The refreshment stops are roughly at a half way point and road walking is kept to an absolute minimum. The Points of Interest add an 'extra' to the day, or should inclement weather prevail, they can provide an alternative to walking.

On a final note, I would like to mention the official map of the 1066 Country Campaign which is available from all 1066 Country Tourist Information Centres. In doing this book of walks, it seemed sensible to link them to many of the places mentioned on this map, thereby offering an even greater choice of things to do and see in a part of Sussex that still elicits a sense of discovery.

EAST SUSSEX

1066 Country

LOCATION OF WALKS

1. Battle to Catsfield
2. Rye to Iden
3. Bodiam to Salehurst
4. Winchelsea to Icklesham
5. Pevensey and Westham
6. Herstmonceux Castle and Wartling
7. Hastings Country Park and Fairlight Glen

8. Fuller's Follies
9. Rye Harbour, Winchelsea Beach and Camber Castle
10. Brede, Powdermill Reservoir and Broad Oak
11. Northiam to Beckley
12. Cooden (Bexhill) and Normans Bay

6

Walk 1

BATTLE TO CATSFIELD

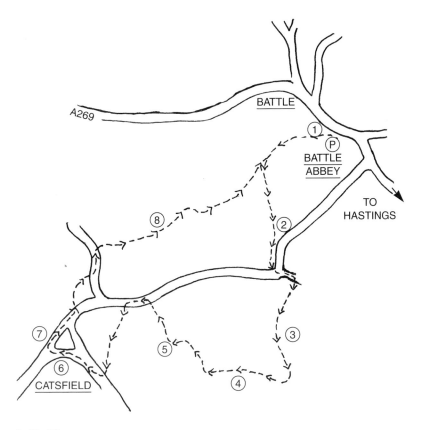

1. Battle
2. Powdermill Lane
3. Peppering Eye Farm
4. Stumblets Wood
5. Wyland Farm
6. Catsfield
7. White Hart Inn
8. Farthings Farm

Walk 1

BATTLE TO CATSFIELD

Distance	Approx 6 miles.
Route	Battle - Powdermill Lane - Peppering Eye Farm - Stumblets Wood - Wyland Farm - Catsfield - White Hart Inn - Farthings Farm - Battle.
Maps	O/S Pathfinder 1290.
Start/Parking	In a Car Park behind Battle Abbey in Battle.
Public Transport	Local Rider 28. County Rider 376, plus various other bus services and British Rail.
Conditions	A fairly easy walk, but can get very muddy after rain, due to heavy soil.
Refreshments	Plenty of choice in Battle. The White Hart, Catsfield.

A visit to the 1066 area simply has to include the heart, Battle and its beautiful rural surroundings. For it was on these hilly slopes that our course of history changed dramatically, when the memorable Battle of Hastings was fought and won by William the Conqueror, all those years ago. It seems almost impossible to imagine that today's peaceful scenery, once witnessed some fourteen thousand soldiers in conflict, fighting to win this country.

Initially the walk covers the perimeter of the battlefield before turning into the delightfully wooded countryside beyond. The many streams and reddish clay soil make it ideal for both water and woodland flowers. It is also good for growing rhododendrons, many of which grace the local cottage gardens. Walking here in the early spring sunshine, beeches and oaks about to burst into leaf, white anemones, ladies mantle and bluebells were particularly in evidence;so too were some fine red foxes, their bushy tails spread behind them. We saw no less than four, including a vixen and her

The Bayeux Tapestry scene showing King Harold's death; contrary to myth, he is probably not the figure with the arrow in his eye. The knight with the dark shield is carrying the Dragon standard of Wessex. A similar design — a monster with wings, three toes, twisted tail and long ears — also appears on the reverse of the Hastings seal.

(*Reproduced with the special authorisation of the town of Bayeux.*)

cub. They presented a charming picture before disappearing with undue haste as they captured scent and sound of my boxer, Jasper, crashing through the undergrowth, oblivious of their presence.

I would suggest a day at Battle should be spent almost exactly as we did. Arriving in the morning to complete the scenic two hour walk to Catsfield, in time to enjoy a well earned lunch at The White Hart. Afterwards the stroll back to Battle along the easy and attractive bridle route, takes about an hour. This allows plenty of time for visiting the Abbey and exploring the historic little town in the afternoon.

Route Directions

On leaving the exit of the Car park behind the Abbey in Battle (1), turn left. Go through the gateway at the end of the lane and follow the fence on the left. This marks the perimeter of the site where the Battle of Hastings took place. Now bear left on reaching a public footpath and a public bridleway sign. Proceed down the hill, keeping to the left. Go through a gate, cross a stream, a stile and a field, eventually arriving in a very muddy and untidy farmyard, which looks more like a graveyard for farm machinery.

At the entrance turn half right, following the top of a bank running parallel with Powdermill Lane (2). Do not attempt to walk along this road,

Battle Abbey.

Battle, from the Abbey walls.

as there is a sharp bend and traffic seems to race round it at an alarming rate. The footpath, which initially is indistinct, ends by a T-junction and a convenient seat.

Now follow the road sign to Crowhurst, taking the first right to Peppering Eye Farm (3). Continue along the tarmac path, past the farm, a rushing spring and finally at a cross section of paths, Stumblets Wood (4) will be on the left and a cottage on the right. Turn right towards a large ugly pylon. Briefly this area becomes scrappy and unattractive, as having passed under the pylon, there are an assortment of dilapidated sheds on the left. At this point the footpath is also narrow and badly kept. Go through a gate, a field, then ignoring the track to the right, walk to the end of another field and turn right into woodland. Cross a footbridge, noting the mass of water iris growing in the shallow waters of the stream. The woodland quickly gives way to yellow gorse and the footpath becomes rather overgrown, however, it soon opens out onto an undulating landscape with a fishing lake to the left.

Continue ahead away from the lake, cross a stile, keep to the right and pass through a gateway. Turn right, then left at another gate and go through Wyland Farm (5), an angling centre. Turn right by a corrugated iron barn, past the fish lakes on either side of the track and turn left having reached a road. Take the next stile on the left and keeping to the left of the field, make for the gate on the far side. To the right the lofty spire of Catsfield Methodist Church comes into view. Walk through the next two fields making for the gate on the left of Catsfield Village School. Turn right along the road to Catsfield (6), bearing left by the church, crossing the road and turning right at the White Hart Inn (7).

Proceed through the village and turn left across a stile, just after a pair of semi-detached bungalows. Having crossed the field and another stile, turn left and continue up the road until arriving at a manor house on one side and a half timbered cottage on the other. Turn right here. There is also a sign indicating a public bridleway. This fairly lengthy but simple route leads all the way back to Battle, first bearing right by Farthings Farm (8), then crossing a stile and ascending rising ground. Finally the bridleway merges with the footpath used at the start of the walk and leads back up the hill to the Car Park.

Points of Interest

Battle

The impressive Abbey Gatehouse, in weathered sandstone, opens on to the winding High Street and a selection of ancient properties, converted shops and restaurants. A haven for browsers. The original town simply consisted of cottages for tradesmen, built at the time and under the protection of, Battle Abbey. Nevertheless, some of the buildings seen today, date from the Elizabethan era and many more merit special interest. Amongst the things to visit are the magnificent St. Mary's Church, erected just east of the Abbey walls, Buckley's Yesterday's World, The Museum of Local History and the Almonery and Town Model.

Catsfield

As Catsfield comes into view on this walk, the exceptionally tall spire of the Methodist Church, appearing over the hill top, dominates the scenery. It is an unusual structure, built by local workmen and containing a tablet in memory of Methodist pioneers. Somewhat sadly, it is now being converted

The White Hart, Catsfield.

into a private dwelling. The 13th century parish church lies south of Catsfield on rising ground, near the school. In the graveyard is the tomb of the famous railway engineer and friend of George Stephenson, Thomas Brassey. The village itself has some attractive properties and is mainly clustered around three roads that form a triangle.

Battle Abbey

The Abbey, now in the care of English Heritage, has been beautifully preserved with detailed information and tableaus, giving a marvellous insight into the significant events of 1066, when the invading Normans, led by William the Conqueror, defeated King Harold and his Saxon army. By tradition the high altar of the church marks the spot where Harold fell. Unfortunately the church, chapter house and part of the cloisters were destroyed when Henry VIII granted the Abbey to Sir Antony Browne, after the dissolution of the monasteries in 1538.

Now the Abbey ruins, including the gatehouse are open throughout the year. Don't forget when visiting, to notice the remarkable views from the terrace across the battlefields to the sea and Beachy Head.

The Gatehouse, Battle Abbey.

Walk 2

RYE TO IDEN

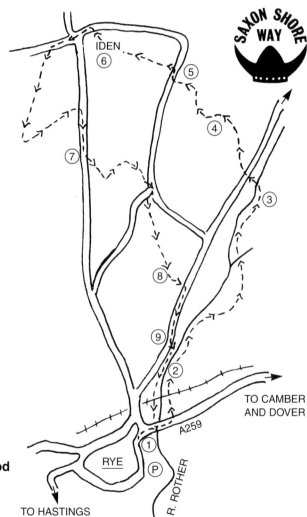

1. Rye
2. River Rother
3. The Lock
4. Houghton Wood
5. Old Turk
6. Iden
7. Iden Road
8. Saltbarn Farm
9. Military Road

Walk 2

RYE TO IDEN

Distance	Approx. 6¼ miles.
Route	Rye - River Rother - The Lock - Houghton Wood - Old Turk - Iden - Iden Road - Saltbarn Farm - Military Road - Rye.
Maps	O/S Pathfinder 1271.
Start/Parking	The walk starts on the far side of the bridge that crosses the River Rother. Parking is in either one of the two small car parks in Rye, just near the A259, Camber and Dover road.
Public Transport	Local Rider 312 and 348, Rye to Iden. Otherwise excellent bus services from all districts to Rye, plus British Rail.
Conditions	Rather exposed along the banks of the River Rother.
Refreshments	The Bell Inn, Iden. Numerous restaurants etc. in Rye.

Picturesque Rye sits on a low hill, south west of the River Rother and the Kent boundary, overlooking marshland, where the sea once rolled. Unfortunately, over a period of time, there has been considerable silting up along this coastline, causing the sea to recede about two miles. In spite of this, Rye still has its quays and a harbour, now used mainly for small boats and its wealth of quaint streets, old houses and crooked chimneys, attract thousands of visitors each year. The romantic and almost medieval atmosphere has made it the favourite haunt of both artists and writers; surely if anywhere was conducive to inspiration, it would be Rye.

However, let's leave the hustle and bustle of the cobbles streets for the peaceful surrounding countryside and a walk that starts and finishes by the

Rother, leaving Rye as a hazy outline topped by a church.

Initially, the route meanders along the river bank, touching a part of the Saxon Shore Way, a walk in itself following the 1066 coastline, starting at Hastings and going beyond Iden Lock into Kent. The marshes to the south east are home to both sheep and a variety of birds; so bring your field glasses if you are an enthusiast. We saw at least a dozen herons in a relatively short space of time, their lumbering, somewhat sluggish lift-off and wide wing span, making them easily recognisable. After crossing the lock, the undulating trail moves amongst farmed fields, hedgerows and trees, with the occasional oast coming into view.

The mellow village of Iden, whose pub provides the halfway refreshment stop, has a shop and a lovely church exhibiting a style of the Norman era. The village is named after Alexander Iden, a past Sheriff of Kent.

The return route passes through the landscape that skirts Playden, before coming back to the river path and a splendid view of the fishing boats, huddled together, moored in the shadows of Rye.

Route Directions

Follow the A259 from Rye (1) until reaching the further side of the bridge that crosses the River Rother (2). There is a sign indicating the Saxon Shore Way. Turn left, following the sign and then pass under the railway bridge. Continue ahead along the towpath, which is also the Sussex Border Path. Cross the Union Channel and make towards some buildings. This is the Lock (3) and having crossed a stile, turn left over the lock itself. Cross the road and footbridge opposite and climb the steps and footpath up the wooded bank a short distance ahead. Traverse a stile turning right, then left, around the perimeter of the field. Turn right by a yellow waymark in the far corner. After the stile, walk through the field diagonally, crossing the stile leading into Houghton Wood (4). Proceed along the footpath, bearing left and then going over a footbridge and stile. Now bear right to a wide gap in the hedge, then keeping the hedge on the left, go towards a fairly large mellow brick property called 'Old Turk' (5). Some oasts are also visible at this point. At the end of the field, climb the stile on the left that is tucked into the hedgerow. Turn right and after one more stile, turn right at the road. Having passed 'Old Turk', go through an iron gate on the left. There

Fishing boats on the Rother at Rye.

'Quizzical sheep', near Rye.

is a waymark. In the far right hand corner of the field cross a stile and keeping to the right of the meadow, proceed until reaching a wide entrance and turn right ignoring the waymark pointing ahead. It is slightly confusing here, as several footpaths meet, so follow directions carefully. Now cross the field to a hedge and stile just over the brow. When we walked here, the field was planted and there was only the barest indication of a footpath. Continue across the next field to a stile by some bungalows, then follow the narrow footpath beyond, turning left at the road into Iden (6).

Carry on past The Bell Inn (unless you are lunching), down Church Lane, turning left up a gravel path to All Saints Church. From the churchyard go through the gate on the far side that opens into the recreation ground and go sharp left to an exceptionally well hidden stile, amongst trees in the corner. With the fence to the left, cross the next stile and a field to a waymarked entrance. Ascend the slope keeping to the left. At the top, by a corrugated shed, turn left up the bridlepath. After a few moments a water tower will appear on the right. Turn right at Iden Road (7).

Continue until reaching a wide track on the left, which looks like the private entrance of a farm. Although there are no waymarks it is a public footpath, so follow it, bearing first left then right after some barns and into a field. Go sharp left. On the far side traverse the stile and staying on the left of the meadowland, turn right at the bottom, past a copse and a cottage. Make for the stile hidden in the corner and turn right along the lane. At a t-junction, cross the green and take the footpath just to the left of a village school. Climb the stile ahead and walk directly across the field to a wide gap in the hedge, then ascend the other side. On reaching Saltbarn Farm (8) and some houses, pass through two iron gates and continue down the track. At Military Road (9) turn right along the wide verge. Carry on for a little less than half a mile. After the sign 'Ancient Rye', a bend in the road and then 'Lorlei House, B&B' on the left. Go left through an iron kissing gate, between a fence and conifers. Turn right on to the towpath by the Rother. Very shortly, the path deviates to pass some houses and a kissing gate. It then crosses the diesel railway line (quite safe) and another kissing gate, finishing at the nearside of the bridge on the A259 at Rye.

Points of Interest

Rye

Throughout the centuries, Rye's fortunes have waxed and waned. Its history has not been a peaceful one. Built on a hill with far reaching views across the channel, it once had heavily fortified walls and guarded the English coast against foreign invasion. It became the target of countless attacks by the French and was plundered, burned and almost reduced to ashes in 1377.

Originally, Rye was conferred on the Abbey of Fechamp, but reclaimed by Henry III in the 13th century. It then entered the confederacy of the Cinque Ports. In the early days, its harbour trade probably consisted mainly of fishing and boat building. Later, during the 15th and 16th centuries, it became a thriving port handling a number of different cargoes, including wool. Thereafter, mostly due to silting up, Rye's prosperity dwindled, although smuggling appeared to provide the local inhabitants with a lucrative income.

Rye today, is a beautifully preserved example of a medieval town, attracting visitors from far and wide. They in turn, gaze in delight at the higgledy piggledy architecture, wander through the winding lanes or browse amongst the shops and potteries. The Tourist Information Centre at Strand Quay has a Rye Town Map which gives details about all the buildings and streets. Guided walks can also be arranged. Listed below are some of the principal things to see:-

a) **Ypres Tower,** housing a Museum. Possibly built by William de Ypres, Earl of Kent, in the 12th century.

b) **Rye Heritage Centre** at Strand Quay.

c) **The Gun Garden,** having extensive views across to Romney Marsh.

d) **St. Mary the Virgin.** A beautiful church with a clock dating from the 16th century. It is said to be one of the oldest, working church clocks in Britain.

e) **Mermaid Street,** with the famous Mermaid Inn, rebuilt in the 15th century after a French raid.

f) **Lamb House,** a Georgian property that used to be the home of the novelist, Henry James. It now belongs to The National Trust and is open from April to October.

g) **Landgate,** once a part of the old town wall.

The Mermaid Inn, Rye.

Walk 3

BODIAM TO SALEHURST

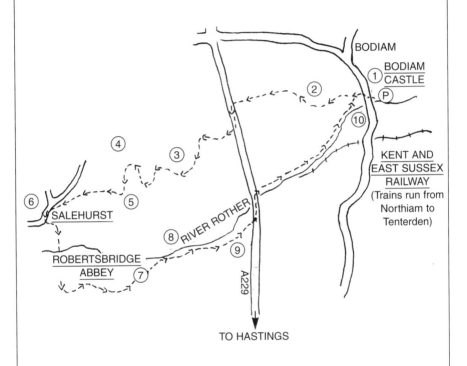

1. Bodiam
2. Knowle Hill
3. Six Acre Wood
4. Higham House
5. Moat Farm
6. Salehurst
7. Robertsbridge Abbey
8. River Rother
9. Udiam Cottages
10. Bodiam Bridge

Walk 3

BODIAM TO SALEHURST

Distance	Approx. 6 miles.
Route	Bodiam - Knowle Hill - Six Acre Wood - Higham House - Moat Farm - Salehurst - Robertsbridge Abbey - River Rother - Udiam Cottages - Bodiam Bridge - Bodiam.
Maps	O/S Pathfinder 1270.
Start/Parking	Bodiam Castle Car Park at southern edge of village.
Public Transport	County Rider 351 from Battle. Local Rider 326/349 from Hastings.
Conditions	A fairly easy walk, the return footpath being on entirely level ground as it follows the banks of the River Rother.
Refreshments	Castle Inn, Bodiam. Salehurst Halt, Salehurst.

The pleasant hillside village of Bodiam, nestling in the trees above its Castle, is somewhat overshadowed by this splendid structure, rising from a broad moat, carpeted with water lilies and filled with fish. The tranquil setting is a world apart from the twentieth century and having returned from the walk to Salehurst, do allow time to visit this fairy tale castle, which although built as a fortress and residence, was never attacked and lived in for over two hundred and fifty years; its complete and perfect outer walls offer a superb example of medieval military architecture and cannot fail to delight the beholder.

This six mile walk travels through some of the loveliest undulating countryside surrounding Bodiam, the nearby River Rother and the tiny hamlet of Salehurst. However, do please note, the outward trail to Salehurst can be tricky as some footpaths appear to have become neglected and in high season, waymarks that have been positioned in fairly obscure places, are often hidden by foliage. Nevertheless, this trail, in spite of any minor difficulties, is amongst the prettiest in Sussex for wild flowers. The hilly slopes and woodland have an abundance of bluebells. There are large areas of wild garlic, their fragile white blooms leaving a pungent odour in the air and the masses of early purple orchids provide short pyramids of colour on the landscape.

The return route is simple and meanders, in most parts, along the reeded banks of the River Rother, having first passed the ruins of Robertsbridge Abbey.

Route Directions

Turn right from the Car Park at Bodiam Castle (1), then left by the side of the Castle Inn. Continue along the lane, through a squeeze gate, past the oasts at Knowle Hill (2), then keeping to the left of some tatty buildings, carry on until reaching a road. Turn left here (there is a wide grass verge to

Bodiam Castle

walk on) and cross the first stile on the right; there is a sign at this point. Ascend the field and cross a stile in the opposite corner. Keep to the left of a large field, called Six Acre Wood (3) and on the far side, pass over a hidden iron footbridge and stile.

Turn right and go through the woodland until reaching a narrow footpath to the left. There is a yellow arrow on the base of a tree at this point, but it is difficult to find, so watch out carefully. Follow the footpath for a short distance, then cross a stile on the right. Staying to the left, go to the second part of the next field, just past a line of trees, and over a stile on the left. Higham House (4) will be on rising ground. Now turn right.

The interior of Bodiam Castle.

Follow the perimeter of the orchards almost down to Moat Farm (5), turn right into a lane then continue straight ahead, through a gate, a field then more orchards. Turn left at the end, then right. Cross the lane, then proceed up the track at the edge of the field, towards Salehurst church. Take the rather overgrown path through the churchyard into Salehurst (6). The Salehurst Halt is on the left.

Leave Salehurst by the bridlepath to the right of the church. Follow it downhill, cross a bridge and turn left, after a gateway, into a lane. The large and lovely house that comes into view on the left is built on the site of Robertsbridge Abbey (7). There are some remaining abbey ruins in the private grounds behind and are easily seen from the bridlepath. Proceed along the lane and through an iron gate. Cross the next three stiles in the foreground and turn right along a footpath that runs parallel with the banks of the River Rother (8). Cross a stile and keep to the left of the meadows by a tributary of the Rother and head towards some red brick houses in a distance; these are Udiam Cottages (9). Just before reaching them, turn left over a footbridge, there is a yellow arrow indicating the way, then go right. Turn left having reached the road and right after the bridge, along the left bank of the Rother. Keep to this winding river footpath until Bodiam Bridge (10) is fairly close. Now bear left across a recreation ground, to the far corner behind the Castle Inn in Bodiam and turn right back to the Car Park.

Points of Interest

Bodiam Castle

The Castle, completed about 1388, was built by Sir Edward Dalyngrigge, initially to protect his vulnerable Manor of Bodiam from raids by the French. In those days, the River Rother was a navigable estuary and therefore, access for the rather too frequent French invaders was a fairly simple task. The attacks never happened and Bodiam Castle became the grand residence for Sir Edward and his family. It was inhabited until the middle of the 17th century, when during the Civil War, much of the interior was despoiled, leaving the ruins open to the winds and weather for three centuries. In 1916 it was purchased and restored by Lord Curzon and it was he who, in 1925, bequeathed it to the National Trust.

Today it remains in their capable hands and the repair and maintenance the Trust carries out, ensures this valuable part of our heritage is well preserved. Bodiam Castle is open to the public throughout the year and there is also a tearoom, shop and Museum.

Salehurst

A tiny hamlet, set deep in the Sussex lanes, just east of Robertsbridge and boasting a fine 13th century church, built by the monks of Robertsbridge. St. Mary's possesses an unusual font, supposedly over seven hundred years old, with a ring of salamanders, a symbol of the Crusaders, around its base. The memorials on the floor near the entrance are of iron, for those who were buried were the family of the local ironmaster.

Robertsbridge Abbey

About half a mile to the south east of Salehurst lie the remains of Robertsbridge Abbey, a Cistercian building, founded in 1176 by Alured de St Martin. The glorious Abbey Farm has some of the old abbey ruins incorporated within its walls, including a rather magnificent archway.

Kent and East Sussex Railway

This minor railway, built at the end of the last century, was not a successful venture. It struggled on until 1954, when the passenger trains were withdrawn and it then operated a goods service only, until 1961 when that too, closed.

In 1973 the Tenterden Railway Company, a registered charity, purchased the derelict line and set about the task of restoration. Now the railway has a varied collection of steam engines with six in full working order, ready to take visitors on the nostalgic journey from Tenterden to Northiam. It is hoped the line will soon be extended to Bodiam and in due course to Robertsbridge, where a link will be made with the main Hastings to Charing Cross railway line.

Locomotive no. 1638 prepares to leave Northiam Station with a train bound for Tenterden on the Kent and East Sussex Railway.

Walk 4

WINCHELSEA TO ICKLESHAM

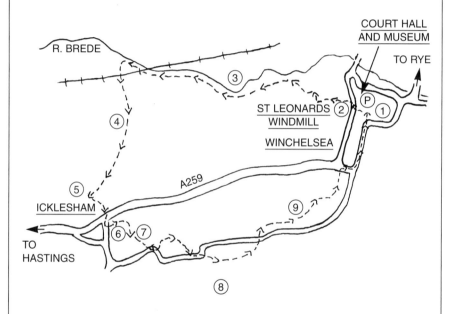

1. Winchelsea
2. St Leonards Windmill
3. River Brede
4. Sheep Wash
5. Icklesham
6. Workhouse Lane
7. Manor Farm Oast
8. Pett Level
9. Wickham Manor

Walk 4

WINCHELSEA TO ICKLESHAM

Distance	Approx 4³/₄ miles.
Route	Winchelsea - St Leonard's Windmill - River Brede - Sheep Wash - Icklesham - Workhouse Lane - Manor Farm Oast - Pett Level - Wickham Manor - Winchelsea.
Maps	O/S Pathfinder 1291.
Start/Parking	In the centre of Winchelsea, near St Thomas' Church, just off the A259, Hastings to Rye road.
Public Transport	Hastings to Folkestone buses 11 and 12.
Conditions	A gentle walk, that can sometimes be wet underfoot in the marshy ground by the River Brede. A word of warning, dogs must be kept on the lead due to large flocks of grazing sheep.
Refreshments	The New Inn, Winchelsea. The Queen's Head Inn, Icklesham.

The areas around Winchelsea and Rye are among my favourite. Here the atmosphere of the past, seems to engulf the surrounding countryside in timeless harmony.

This lovely gentle walk leaves the historic hilltop town of Winchelsea, passes the ruins of St. Leonards Windmill and meanders through the marshes, either side of the River Brede. An assortment of birdlife inhabits the reeded streams and low-lying scrub. Then there are sheep, hundreds and hundreds of them, grazing in the lush meadows of varying hues.

We chose a fascinating time to walk in these parts, for the April lambing was at its height and the newborn youngsters regarded us playfully,

Winchelsea with St Thomas Church in the background.

quizzically and without fear. We witnessed a ewe in the latter stages of giving birth and interestingly, on nearing, about twelve sheep moved forward and surrounded her, thus forming a protective barrier against unwelcome strangers. Six more sheep then lined up behind us and as we walked away, followed, hot on our heels, just to make sure we were really leaving. Another ewe, nuzzling a lamb that couldn't have been more than an hour old, stamped her foot angrily at our unwanted intrusion during such a private moment. Who says sheep are silly?

The gardens of The Queen's Head Inn proved a very pleasant viewpoint, showing the rich valley of the Brede, leading towards Winchelsea then Rye.

We wandered on southwards, past the church at Icklesham, over the brow of the hill, through apple orchards and towards the fringes of the exposed marshes at Pett Level. Beyond lay the sea.

A prominent landmark at this point is a well kept windmill. It is situated in the private grounds of an unusual almost circular house, perhaps the miller's at one time, and commands splendid views across the coastline.

On returning to Winchelsea the stone built, New Gate, comes into view. A few hundred years ago the only access to the town was via one of the three medieval gateways. The remains still stand. Strand Gate on the eastern side is the best preserved and has a 'look-out' adjacent to the walls. On an exceptionally clear day it is possible to see France from here.

Route Directions

From the church at the centre of Winchelsea (1), walk down the road by the side of The New Inn, turn right at the end, then first left down a lane. Go through a gate towards the ruins of St Leonards Windmill (2). Pass over the gate beyond, bearing right down the hill on a sunken path and traverse the stile. Turn left crossing the next stile and footbridge then, having gone over another stile, turn left along the banks of the River Brede (3). The scenery is now dominated by sheep.

Continue along the towpath until reaching a railway line, which incidentally is diesel, not electric, so it is safe to cross, but look both ways. Proceed over the stile, railway line and stile. Go to the footbridge, turn left and repeat the exercise of crossing a stile, railway line and stile, but I hasten to add, in a different place to the previous one. Go through the gate beyond

St Thomas Church.

The remains of the medieval 'New Gate'.

and the Sheep Wash (4) will be on the right. Icklesham Church is also clearly visible. Carry on to a stile, then a gate and yet another gate, finishing at the foot of the hill leading to Icklesham (5). Climb the slope, bearing right. Do not follow the bridlepath ahead. At the top of the hill, cross a stile, a field and a stile leading into the gardens of The Queen's Head. The name is painted on the roof, so it is very easy to see and makes an ideal place to stop for lunch.

Using the main entrance from the pub, bear left down the lane. Cross the road into Workhouse Lane (6) and almost immediately take the first left to Icklesham Church. Do try and find time to visit this charming little church. Now follow the footpath sign at the rear of the churchyard, just before the stile and turn left. Keep on the path, with the fence on the left, to Manor Farm Oast (7), the oasts are very easy to see. Stay to the right of them and continue onwards for a short distance before turning left through a wire gate into apple orchards. Walk between the orchards, the way is signed, then leave by a gate on the right at the far end. Turn left, go left again over a stile and cross a large field behind a disused windmill, to a gate on the other side. Turn left and traverse a stile at the corner of the road ahead. Proceed across the field. From this point are the most wonderful views to the marshy Pett

Levels (8) and the sea; Dungeness also stands out clearly on the horizon.

Move on through the next stile and field, heading for the gate in the far left corner and cross the road and stile facing. Continue via two more fields to a stile on the right of Wickham Manor (9) and then cross the stile and field opposite. Go to the gate in the bottom left corner. The old Town Gate will be on the right. Climb the hill to a stile about half way along the hedgerow and turn left up a bridleway. Turn right, then left along the road back to Winchelsea.

Points of Interest

Winchelsea

13th century Winchelsea, once referred to as a 'town in a trance, dreaming of centuries gone by'; a description that suits it to perfection.

However, this was not the first Winchelsea, the earlier one lies about three miles to the south-east, buried under sand and destroyed by violent storms, high tides and erosion.

Historically, this little port was of great importance to the realm. Therefore it was considered necessary to lend national funds to rebuild such a place, but this time on a safer site at the nearby Iham Hill.

The plans for New Winchelsea were on an ambitious scale. They included thirty nine squares, the roads criss-crossing at more or less right angles, an enormous church, a town hall, wine cellars, an abbey and to the north, the port. It became a thriving medieval town.

Unfortunately, it did not enjoy its wealth and prosperity for long. By the fifteenth century, after constant raids by the French and the plague, the port began silting up. Slowly Winchelsea started to decline.

Today it is a mere skeleton of its former self, but what is left is charming, picturesque and steeped in history. There is also plenty for the visitor to see, although not immediately apparent when simply passing through. A detailed guide, available from St. Thomas Church, will ensure that none of the sights or information about them, are missed.

The Court Hall and Museum

Opposite St. Thomas Church, on a corner, stands the 14th century, or possibly even earlier, Court Hall. Its lower part was once the town gaol. the upper part now houses the local museum and contains some fascinating exhibits. It is open to the public throughout the summer.

St. Leonard's Windmill

Sadly this windmill was destroyed in the storm of 1987. All that remains is the base, the outlines of brick walls and a large grinding stone. It was originally built in 1703 on the site of the ancient Saxon church of St. Leonard's.

Icklesham

A village whose name originates from Saxon times and means 'the homestead of Icel', is one of the earliest places to have been inhabited by the Normans, after they seized the peninsula east of Hastings. The attractive All Saints Church offers early to late Norman features with some fine carvings at the tops of the pillars. On the north wall, an old notice board bears details of two ancient charities within the parish; The Cheney Trust of Almshouses in Icklesham and Guestling and the John Fray bequest of 1592.

The Queens Head, Icklesham.

Walk 5

PEVENSEY AND WESTHAM

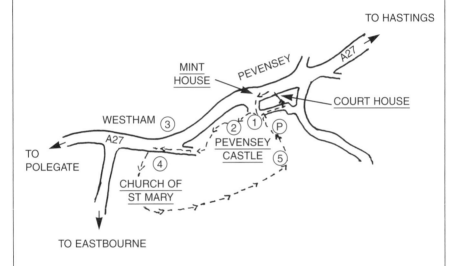

1. Pevensey
2. Pevensey Castle
3. Westham
4. Church of St. Mary
5. Anderida

Walk 5

PEVENSEY AND WESTHAM

Distance	Approx. 1^1/$_2$ miles.
Route	Pevensey - Pevensey Castle - Westham - St. Mary's Church - Anderida - Pevensey.
Maps	O/S Pathfinder 1309.
Start/Parking	At the Car Park in Pevensey on the eastern side of Pevensey Castle.
Public Transport	28 Eastbourne to Rye. 99 Eastbourne to Hastings. British Rail to Westham.
Conditions	A short stroll that could be wet underfoot after the church, on the way back to Pevensey.
Refreshments	The Pevensey Castle, Westham. Priory Court, The Royal Oak and The Smugglers Inn, Pevensey.

The walk between Pevensey and Westham is not a long one, but it covers one of the most importantly placed stretches of coastline in our history. In Roman times it acted as a harbour and stronghold against the Saxons and it was here that William the Conqueror landed on that well known date of 1066, marking the beginning of the Norman invasion of England.

The Roman fort of Anderida, frequently referred to as the outer walls of Pevensey Castle, was built around 340 AD. At that time Pevensey was a peninsula, the inlet of the sea extending as far back as Hailsham. Part of this walk crosses the marshland at the foot of Anderida, where the sea once broke against the irregular fort walls and boats juddered at their moorings.

It is easy to let the imagination run riot when wandering here, or in the castle precincts. Especially when a mist creeps inland, nudging the castle turrets and the damp silence makes you look over your shoulder and wonder if it was a spirit from a bygone era that brushed fleetingly past. Was that noise the stealthy step of a smuggler? Happily it is only imagination, although it could have been fact during the 17th century, when smuggling provided the local inhabitants with a very profitable sideline.

Within a little more than a mile, Pevensey and Westham can offer the visitor a Roman fort, a Norman castle, 15th century buildings, two churches (one of them being Norman), a 14th century Mint House and an old Court House and Gaol. What more can you ask for?

Route Directions

From the Car Park at Pevensey (1), enter the castle grounds by the eastern arch, opposite the Royal Oak and Castle Inn. Go through the gate and follow the path by the side of the moat and Pevensey Castle (2). Then continue across the precincts to the gate on the western edge, leading into Westham (3). Pass through the gate, into the lane beyond and carry on until reaching the Norman church of St. Mary's (4). Turn left into the churchyard through the Sussex squeeze gate. However, before you do this, walk on a little further to look at Westham High Street, the Oak House and the old Dial House, both 15th century.

Now return to the churchyard, proceed by the side of the church keeping the hedge to the left at the end, then right, crossing the footbridge in the far corner of the graveyard and turn left. Keeping to the left, continue across the area of marshland and from here are some splendid views of Anderida (5), the Roman fort. Cross a blue footbridge, turn left and go through the gate ahead, which leads into Pevensey Car Park. Now turn right down the lane that runs between the two parking areas, turn left opposite St. Nicholas Church and follow the sign to the 'Court House and Gaol'. Turn left by the Court House, back into Pevensey, noting Banks Lodge with an interesting cobbled facia and The Old Mint House opposite the Car Park.

Points of Interest

Pevensey Castle

At the Norman Conquest, Pevensey was granted to William the Conqueror's half-brother, the Count of Mortain. It was he who established

Elizabethan demi-culverin at Pevensey Castle.

The Normans built their castle in the south-east corner of the Roman fort at Pevensey. The gatehouse at the left of the picture contains some original work but the curtain wall and drum tower to the right were built in the mid-13th century.

the village of Pevensey outside the old Roman fort of Anderida and erected the fortified castle within the already crumbling walls. Substantial repairs had to be made to these, which by then were seven hundred years old. The castle itself was altered or added to, over the next three hundred years. It was beseiged no less than four times and fell into the possession of various notable families. This probably partially depended on who had found favour with the King. Access to the Roman fort is possible throughout the year, owing to the public footpath that runs through the grounds. The castle is open from March until October.

The Church of St. Mary, Westham

This claims to be the first church the Normans built after the landing at Pevensey in 1066. Possibly there was a Saxon church here, prior to this date. If so, it was demolished by the Normans, which they did with so many churches, in order to rebuild their own bigger and better edifice. Part of the Norman structure remains today; the rest stems from different eras, including a massive 15th century font, constructed from local greenstone.

The Court House and Gaol

Pevensey Court House is now a museum. The building dates from the latter part of the 16th century, although a Court House has stood on this site since 1207. It consists of a courtroom, a robing room, two cells and a tiny exercise yard. It was the smallest Town Hall in England and today contains many interesting exhibits and maps.

The Mint House

This intriguing half timbered house, standing in the shadows of the castle, is over six hundred years old. It is built on the site of a Norman Mint, that was in use from 1076 until 1154. Some examples of the coins struck here are in the British Museum. The present house was considerably altered in 1542, when Dr. Andrew Borde, Physician to King Henry VIII lived in it. There are eighteen rooms to see including one, which is panelled with oak carvings from the Renaissance period and another, which is apparently haunted.

Walk 6

HERSTMONCEUX CASTLE AND WARTLING

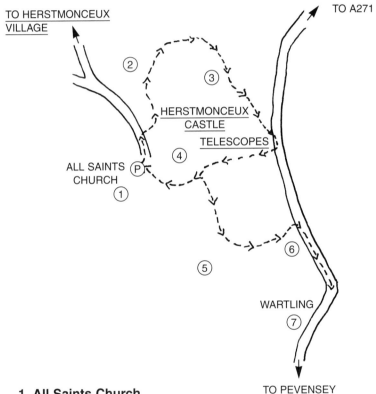

1. All Saints Church
2. Herstmonceux Place
3. The Park
4. Herstmonceux Castle
5. Pevensey Marshes
6. Coopers Farm
7. Wartling

Walk 6

HERSTMONCEUX CASTLE AND WARTLING

Distance	Circular route of the Herstmonceux estate - approx. $2^1/_4$ miles.
	Non-circular deviation to Wartling - approx. 2 miles.
Route	All Saints Church - Herstmonceux Place - The Park - Herstmonceux Castle - Pevensey Marshes - Coopers Farm - Wartling - Herstmonceux Castle - All Saints Church.
Maps	O/S Pathfinder 1290 and 1309.
Start/Parking	In the lane by All Saints Church, about two miles from Herstmonceux village. This is reached by following the signs to Flowers Green from the A 271.
Public Transport	98 Bus from Eastbourne to Hastings, stopping at Herstmonceux village.
Conditions	Parts of the walk could be muddy during wet weather, especially the Pevensey marsh area.
Refreshments	The Lamb Inn, Wartling. Selection of pubs and restaurants in Herstmonceux.

This delightful walk encircles, first the Herstmonceux Estate, then offers the choice of either extending the trail to include the pretty hamlet of Wartling, or alternatively , visiting the 15th century castle grounds - (there is an entrance charge to do this). If, of course, one wishes to spend the day in the beautiful surroundings made famous in 1066, what could be more enjoyable than doing all those things mentioned?

The footpath wanders through the woods and fields bordering Herstmonceux Castle and every so often, there is a rewarding glimpse of this moated brick edifice, lying in a secluded south-facing position. The curious domes of the Equatorial Telescope buildings are also passed; these too can be visited. The woodland areas yield a variety of magnificent trees, including, Horse Chestnut, Sweet Chestnut, Maple and Oak. In places, it is still possible to see the remains of an avenue, suggesting that there may have been other carriageways to the castle. Now, nature has taken over, and brambles and bracken have encroached across the wide paths.

When William the Conqueror set foot on these shores, Wartling overlooked the sea. Today, even the most inexperienced eye can visualize the marshy Pevensey Levels being a large estuary and harbour. Part of the path to Wartling follows the old coastline, before branching off through a stretch of farmland.

Route Directions

From All Saints Church (1), proceed northwards, back up the road and take the footpath through the second gate on the right; the sign indicates Windmill Hill. Continue straight along the woodland track, ignoring a bridlepath crossroads, until reaching an iron gate. The imposing Herstmonceux Place (2) will be on the left. Go down the field beyond and bear right; there is a blue waymark sited here. Pass through the meadow, turning right at the iron gate near the end. Follow the attractively avenued woodland track until a heavily reeded pond is reached. This entire area is known as 'The Park' (3). After the pond, turn right along a signed footpath, across a wooden footbridge, over a stile, then cross the next field diagonally. The domes of the Equatorial Group of Telescopes can be seen on the right. Cross the stile in the far corner by some trees and turn right along Wartling Road. Almost immediately, the tourist brown sign, showing the entrance to Herstmonceux Castle (4) appears. If you wish to visit the Castle grounds, now is the time to do so.

Just past the sign, turn right and keeping to the right, take the bridlepath at the end of the car park and continue along the edge of woodland, until reaching an iron gate. Note the fabulous views of Herstmonceux Castle that keep appearing amongst the trees on the right. Go into the field beyond the gate, past a huge tree stump, to a wooden right of way sign.

Herstmonceux Castle.

The Equatorial Group of Telescopes.

At this point turn left for the deviation to Wartling (see below), or continue the circular route, past the Castle and through the gate ahead. Follow the track up the slope and after the next gate, cross a road to the lane opposite and turn right back to All Saints Church, having passed some garage buildings on the right.

For Wartling

From the wooden sign, turn left through the field and cross a stile. Ignore the immediate path on the right by a stream. Instead, turn right by the line of trees a short distance ahead and follow their perimeter. This was the old coastline in 1066. There are yellow waymarks, but the track is barely discernible, partially due to the constant activity of sheep grazing on the lush and often muddy fringes of Pevensey Marshes (5). Cross a stile and keep to the left, bearing left over a secluded stile. Traverse another stile, turn left, cross the stile ahead and walk towards Cooper's Farm (6). Go through two iron gates, past the farmyard buildings and turn right along the road into Wartling (7). From here, it is a mere quarter of a mile to this pretty hamlet and The Lamb Inn; but take care, although it's only a country lane, it can sometimes be busy. However, there is a wide grass verge to walk along.

Return by the same route to the wooden sign in front of Herstmonceux Castle.

Points of Interest

Herstmonceux Castle

Hertsmonceux Castle sits on the site of the old Manor of 'Herste', which used to form part of the lands of Count d'Eu, one of the Conqueror's generals. It is thought to be one of the oldest brick buildings in England. It was constructed in the 15th century by Sir Roger Fiennes and seems to combine his love of the French brick chateau, an English castle and a stylish country mansion, culminating in a splendid, yet almost folly-like structure, with a wealth of towers and battlements. On his death in 1449, it passed to his son Richard, who married Joan, grandaughter of Thomas, the 6th Lord Dacre. It remained in the family until 1708, when it was sold to a George Naylor for £38,215. The castle then passed through his family, finally falling into disrepair and in 1776, after a sale of the contents, it was demolished, leaving only the outer walls and the gate-house intact.

During the next hundred and fifty years, the castle estate had a succession of owners, several of them opening the ruins to visitors and charging 6d. In 1936, the building was completely restored to its former glory by Sir Paul Latham M.P. and in 1946, the entire estate was purchased by the Admiralty, to be the new home of The Royal Observatory, Greenwich. Just recently, in 1993, it was bought by Queens University, Ontario, Canada.

Equatorial Group of Telescopes

The Royal Observatory was founded at Greenwich in 1675. By the twentieth century, London pollution made astronomical observation increasingly difficult and the new site of Herstmonceux was chosen. The move took ten years to complete. Sadly, during the mid seventies, pollution caught up with the Observatory once more, necessitating yet another move, this time to the Canary Islands.

A Science Centre is now housed in the Equatorial Telescope buildings, which have also become quite a famous landmark.

Herstmonceux Village

Herstmonceux has a parish of some thirty odd miles in circumference, the All Saints Church being two miles from the centre. It is an exceptionally attractive church and on the chancel floor lies a superb brass to the memory of Sir William Fiennes, whose son Roger built the Castle.

The village itself has a number of interesting 15th and 16th century properties, all with a long history, including a house known as Bedlam Cottage, because it used to be the old lunatic asylum. Unfortunately, many of the buildings cannot be appreciated due to the amount of traffic that appears to clog the main street. However, there are some fascinating shops to browse in and it is also where the Sussex Trug, a slatted wooden basket, has been made for the last hundred and sixty years.

The brass to the memory of Sir William Fiennes at All Saints Church.

Walk 7

HASTINGS COUNTRY PARK AND FAIRLIGHT GLEN

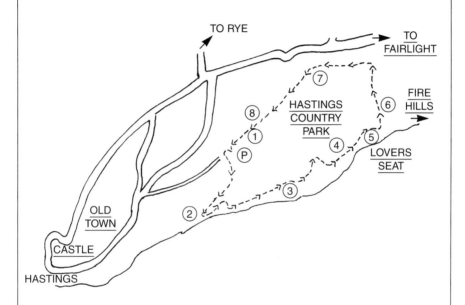

1. Shear Barn Farm
2. Ecclesbourne Glen
3. Covehurst Wood
4. Fairlight Glen
5. Lovers Seat
6. Coastguard Cottages
7. Fairlight Place
8. Barley Lane

Walk 7

HASTINGS COUNTRY PARK AND FAIRLIGHT GLEN

Distance	Approx 3¹/₂ miles.
Route	Shear Barn Farm - Ecclesbourne Glen - Covehurst Wood - Fairlight Glen - Lover's Seat -Coastguard Cottages - Fairlight Place - Barley Lane - Shear Barn Farm.
Maps	O/S Pathfinder 1291.
Start/Parking	The Car Park by Shear Barn Farm, reached by following the brown signs to 'Shear Barn Caravan Park', from Hastings Old Town.
Public Transport	44/344 Hastings, Fairlight and Rye. Local Rider 345.
Conditions	Some steep climbing along the cliff tops which can be muddy and slippery after rain.
Refreshments	The Barn Tearoom at Fairlight Place (when open). The Ecclesbourne, on the Hastings side of Shear Barn Car Park. Alternatively, a picnic.

The sweeps, curves and vistas of the coastline at Hastings Country Park, give yet another different and rewarding aspect of the Sussex panorama. Here the soil is sandy, encouraging close growing oaks in the wooded valleys that hug the seashore. Beneath the trees lie tiny streams banked by bracken, mosses and lichen. Gorse, elder and blackberries take over the sunny positions, the latter bearing masses of purple fruit in the autumn.

I personally feel this walk warrants a picnic; even on a windy day, the glens and coves offer sheltered spots, where one could sit and enjoy the

Looking towards Ecclesbourne Glen.

The cliffs near Fairlight.

uninterrupted scenery with adequate protection. A good half-way picnic place would be on the beach at Fairlight Glen, a short distance from the circular path and mentioned in Route Directions.

It is perfectly possible to extend this walk either to the west, just beyond Ecclesbourne Glen, or to the east, finishing at Fire Hills, near Fairlight Cove. It is all exceptionally well signed, so one is unlikely to get lost. However, do remember that there is a lot of steep uphill trekking which can be tiring.

Route Directions

Take the footpath in the left corner of the Car Park by Shear Barn Farm (1) and head directly down the valley. Descend some steps, cross a stream and on reaching a meeting of footpaths, with a rather neglected central wooden sign, follow the track opposite. Continue ahead until the path opens out on to the cliff tops and another wooden sign. The sweeping coastal valley of Ecclesbourne Glen (2), will be on the right.

Turn left, proceed uphill, then turn right by a yellow waymark and a wooden fence. Follow the cliff path, Covehurst Wood (3) and the sea will

'*Curiosity*'.

be on the right. Start descending after a short while into Fairlight Glen (4). There is a waymark. Go down some steps, past another sign and continue through the trees and scrub until reaching the bottom of the glen. Follow the sign that indicates access to the beach but carry on past the steps and spring leading to it. Proceed uphill, turning right near the top, up more steps which will culminate on the cliffs and the spot claimed to be 'Lover's Seat' (5). After another lot of steps, the vista opens out and the Coastguard Cottages (6) at Fairlight can be seen on the cliffs ahead.

Now turn left along the uphill path away from the coast, keeping the fence on the right. Cross a stile at the top, turn left and go over another stile. Cross the field and two more stiles. Keep to the footpath, traversing two further stiles on the way. Having reached a kissing gate, Fairlight Place (7) will be on the left. Take the footpath opposite. This is Barley Lane (8) and leads back to the Car Park by Shear Barn Farm.

Points of Interest

Hastings Country Park

This beautiful Country Park stretches from East Hill in Hastings to Cliff End near Pett. From the fishermans' quarter in Hastings, it can be reached by using the steep East Hill Cliff Railway, or if you're feeling fit, climbing numerous steps.

The Park covers 260 hectares; the geology is unique as the terrain varies from grassland to heathland, woodland and seashore. It was opened in 1974 by the Hastings Borough Council and is designated as a site of special scientific interest.

Lover's Seat

Presumably there was once an actual seat on this romantic cliff top locality; or could it have been the large flat rock almost hidden amongst the gorse? Whatever, it is said that if you 'plight your troth' at this point, you'll live happily ever after.

This charming thought is based on the 18th century tale of two lovers whose parents strongly disapproved of their match and went to great lengths to end it. The girl was sent to live on a remote farm and her lover, a naval captain from Rye, sailed his cutter up and down the coast, waiting for her to signal her whereabouts. She did, from Lover's Seat and their runaway marriage followed her escape, with the cutter's crew acting as look-outs. According to legend, a reconciliation with the parents was effected soon after the wedding.

Fairlight

The hamlet of Fairlight consists of a few strung out properties, a church, coastguard cottages and a Visitor Centre in the Car Park. St. Andrews, sited amongst trees has an exceptionally tall tower and was built in 1845 in the Gothic style.

Fire Hills

The gorse covered cliffs beyond Fairlight, that turn a brilliant yellow in spring, are known as Fire Hills. Supposedly, they were named by ancient seafarers passing in their ships.

Hastings Castle and Old Town

Don't leave this area without visiting William the Conqueror's 900-year-old castle, perched high on a rocky cliff, with the narrow streets and twittens of Old Town criss-crossing the hill below. This ruined, yet atmospheric castle with magnificent views, has a medieval seige tent where, with the help of sound and projected images, one can watch and listen to the 1066 story.

In the 1066 free information on Hastings, there is a detailed map of Old Town; included is an excellent walk, marked in red and showing all the places of interest in this ancient locality.

Walk 8

FULLER'S FOLLIES

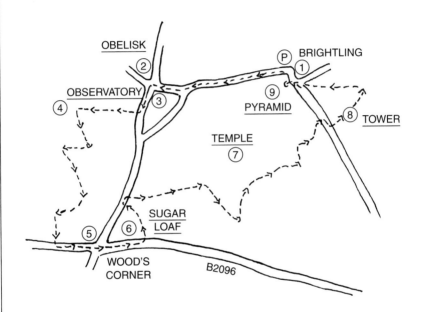

1. **Brightling**
2. **The Obelisk**
3. **The Observatory**
4. **Brightling Down**
5. **Wood's Corner**
6. **The Sugar Loaf**
7. **The Temple**
8. **The Tower**
9. **The Pyramid**

Walk 8

FULLER'S FOLLIES

Distance	Approx. 5$^1/_2$ miles.
Route	Brightling - The Obelisk - The Observatory - Brightling Down - Wood's Corner - The Sugar Loaf - The Temple - The Tower - The Pyramid - Brightling.
Maps	O/S Pathfinders 1290 & 1270.
Start/Parking	At the side of the churchyard in Brightling; a mile and a half from the B 2096 at Wood's Corner.
Public Transport	Local Rider 355 from Battle to Heathfield.
Conditions	A hilly walk but nothing too strenuous.
Refreshments	The Swan Inn, Wood's Corner.

A larger than life character, associated with Sussex, John Fuller of Brightling (1757-1834), must rank amongst the most eccentric. Known as 'Honest Jack', 'Mad Jack' and 'Hippopotamus', on account of his twenty-two stone, he left a wealth of legends and a range of follies for people to ponder over and gaze upon.

He was descended from a family whose fortunes were made by acquiring land and property in the 16th century. Thereafter, an interest in the Sussex iron industry proved a profitable venture and by the time John Fuller was born, the money that had been made was invested, assuring him of a secure and comfortable future.

He was orphaned when a boy and at the age of twenty, inherited everything and took possession of the family home, Rose Hill at Brightling, adjacent to the church. At the beginning of the nineteenth century, he became an M.P. and his outspoken personality frequently got him into trouble; especially when he referred to the Speaker as 'That insignificant man in a wig'. John Fuller's political career ended in 1810; he then concentrated on his interests in the arts and science. He never married, although almost inevitably, a character such as his, has collected numerous risque tales.

This 'Folly Spotting' walk is not only great fun, it also covers the rolling meadows and woodlands of the High Weald, one of the most beautiful regions of Sussex. If possible, try and chose a fine clear day to do this ramble, as the panorama is magnificent. Looking southward, it stretches from Beachy Head to the Downs at Firle Beacon, then travels round towards Lewes. In the east, on returning to Brightling, one can see the Darwell Reservoir, Bodiam Castle and across the countryside to Kent.

Route Directions

From the churchyard and telephone kiosk in Brightling (1), continue westwards along the road past the wall of Brightling Park. At a fork, follow the road sign indicating Burwash; the Obelisk (2) will appear on the right. At the next crossroads, turn left along the lane leading to the domed Observatory (3). Turn right just past this building, by a reservoir, and go through an iron gate along the bridlepath. About halfway down an incline, turn left onto a footpath and having reached a field, cross to the yellow waymark positioned on a tree. Now carry straight on to a stile and further sign. This whole area is called Brightling Down (4). Cross the stile and turn right. Keep to the left of the field and traverse a stile on the left, leading into woodland. Turn left immediately on to a narrow, slightly overgrown path, crossing a footbridge and proceed through the woods until entering a field. Please note, this next bit of the walk can be tricky, so follow the route directions carefully.

Carry on ahead, keeping to the left. After the second part of the field, there will be a cattle trough on the left. Turn right here, along the hedgerow and descend this field, following the perimeter until reaching a gap in the trees at the bottom. Turn right across a slatted type of fence; cross flat, slightly boggy ground, then bearing right, ascend the field beyond, with the hedge on the left. Climb over a stile at the top of the hill, by a converted barn and go left up a tarmac lane, turning left again at the main road, towards Wood's Corner (5). Continue along the footpath and the Swan Inn will be on the right.

The Temple.

Having passed the Swan Inn and a garage, take the signed footpath on the left leading to the Sugar Loaf (6) after which make for the gap in the hedge ahead and follow a narrow footpath. Turn left by a wood yard, right onto a road, then immediately right through a brick gateway into a forest. Proceed down the wide path until reaching a sort of T-junction. At this point the Temple (7) will be on the hill in front. Bear right and having turned a corner, take the steep track on the left, crossing a footbridge before climbing the bank opposite. Continue through the next two gates towards a copse, then follow the footpath to the left of it. From here are some excellent views of the Temple. After what appears to be a pheasant breeding pen and an iron gate, cross the next two fields to a bridlepath that bears right between farm buildings, then left past some ponds. Follow the bridletrack uphill towards the Tower (8). Turn right at the road and left at the signed footpath, which passes round the base of the Tower, into the field beyond and turns left by the hedgerow at the bottom. After the kissing gate, continue through the next two fields, cross the lane and make for Fuller's Pyramid (9) in the churchyard at Brightling.

Points of Interest

The Brightling Needle

The Needle, or Obelisk at 65 foot high, stands atop Brightling Beacon, one of the highest points in Sussex. It is situated on private land, but is easily visible from the road and provides a prominent landmark for many miles.

The Observatory

This domed building used to be a working observatory, housing the advanced equipment necessary for John Fuller's much loved hobby, astronomy. It was designed by his friend, the well known architect, Sir Robert Smirke and the building was completed by 1818. After Fuller's death, It was used for a number of things, including a museum. It is now a private residence.

The Sugar Loaf

A curious conical structure, standing at 35 feet high, near Wood's Corner. Legend says Fuller wagered Dallington church spire could be seen from his home, Rose Hill at Brightling. When he found he was wrong, he erected a building of a similar shape, thus enabling him to win the wager.

The Temple

Sited on sloping ground in the middle of Brightling Park, the Rotunda Temple is 25 feet high, circular, domed with classical pillars. It is thought to have been designed by Sir Robert Smirke and possibly dates from about

The Tower.   *The Sugar Loaf.*

1810. As to its use, nobody is sure. It has been suggested that it could have been the place where Fuller entertained his lady friends.

The Tower

This single tower, built of stone, is 35 feet high and sits amongst gorse and trees a short distance from the road. The legend attached to this folly says Fuller may have had it built when he purchased Bodiam Castle in 1828. The castle needed much restoration and to make sure the work progressed satisfactorily, he kept a watchful eye on it, from the top of the Tower.

The building can be visited today and the view is well worth the climb up the iron staircase.

The Pyramid

When John Fuller died on April 11th 1834, he was interred under his Pyramid in Brightling churchyard. It seems however, that even after his death, the outrageous stories still followed him. It was said he had been buried in his 25 ft mausoleum, seated in a chair, wearing a top hat and clutching a bottle of claret. In reality, he lay recumbent beneath the floor.

The Pyramid in Brightling churchyard.

Walk 9

RYE HARBOUR, WINCHELSEA BEACH & CAMBER CASTLE

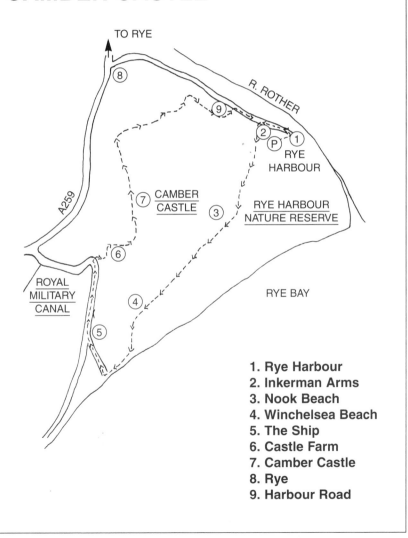

1. Rye Harbour
2. Inkerman Arms
3. Nook Beach
4. Winchelsea Beach
5. The Ship
6. Castle Farm
7. Camber Castle
8. Rye
9. Harbour Road

Walk 9

RYE HARBOUR, WINCHELSEA BEACH & CAMBER CASTLE

Distance	Approx 6 miles.
Route	Rye Harbour - Inkerman Arms - Nook Beach - Winchelsea Beach - The Ship - Castle Farm - Camber Castle - Rye - Harbour Road - Rye Harbour.
Maps	O/S Pathfinder 1291.
Start/Parking	The Car Park at Rye Harbour.
Public Transport	Local Rider 345, from Rye.
Conditions	A level coastal walk, but very exposed, so don't try it on a very windy day.
Refreshments	The Ship, Winchelsea Beach. The Inkerman Arms and The Conqueror at Rye Harbour.

A very different, yet timeless walk across the lonely marshland between Rye and Winchelsea. Here the mist can edge in, wreathing itself silently amongst the reeded waterways: or the wind can buffet against you as it blows across the English Channel, sending the seabirds wheeling and crying into a leaden sky. Alternatively, a blue sky and hot sun may cause a heat haze to shimmer on the flat, watery horizon and the warmth will make the clumps of yellow-horned sea poppies bloom in profusion.

Almost the entirety of this walk takes place within the Rye Harbour Nature Reserve, a delight for birdwatchers. We encountered such a group, field glasses trained on the antics of a bird. Jasper, our dog, greeted them effusively. Understandably, they were not as effusive as he at the sudden intrusion, which caused whatever it was to fly away. Slightly embarrassed, we moved on, Jasper in tow. A lesson learned; keep over friendly dogs on the lead.

The unusual single storey, minuscule houses at Winchelsea Beach appear to have come from a 1930's film set; they have a curious charm, many of them made from shiplap, with an odd converted railway carriage amongst them. They sit close to the sea wall on shingle, surrounded by elder and the feathery pink flowers of tamarisk.

The 16th century Camber Castle lies in isolated splendour in the middle of the marshes. In some ways it is a pity that it's only accessible by the walker; on the other hand, perhaps that's part of it's charm. The atmosphere is one of solitude, with only the gulls who inhabit the abandoned stone walls, as companions. Between the castle and Rye lies the Royal Military Canal Path, a trail in itself, following the Royal Military Canal.

The final part of this walk is not so attractive as it passes a small industrial area. Nevertheless, it is only for a short time, so don't let it put you off spending an unusual and rewarding day in the Rye Harbour Nature Reserve.

Route Directions

Leave the Car Park at Rye Harbour (1) with the Martello Tower on the right. Turn left and left again down the main street. Go left at a wide entrance. just after The Inkerman Arms (2). This turns into a bridlepath and initially passes corrugated sheds and other rather untidy constructions. Continue along the shingled track, passing an extensive area of man made

A threatening sky over Rye Harbour.

59

'puddles', called 'Nook Beach' (3), for two and a half miles. Bear left after a slight incline, making towards some bungalows. Proceed along the path, finally bearing left on to the sea wall at Winchelsea Beach (4). From here the views are amazing. Great long stretches of first, shingle then sand, continuing right up to Dungeness on the left and Fairlight and Hastings to the right. Walk along the sea wall, turning right at some steps, by a public loo. Go down the road beyond, keeping to the right at a fork. 'The Ship' (5) will be on the right after a short distance.

Boats at Rye Harbour.

From the pub turn right along the road, turning right again at a sharp corner. Take the shingle track, turning right by some farm buildings and left by Castle Farm (6). Go through the gate, take the left track and continue towards Camber Castle (7), crossing a stile to the left of it. Fork right and take the grass track around the castle itself, then head away to the left, towards Rye (8). Traverse a stile and continue ahead crossing another stile. Go over yet another stile and bear sharply left. Turn right at the end of a fence. There are waymarks along this part of the walk, which has a rather unattractive industrial area to the left. Follow the overgrown trail between various bits of waterways until reaching a gateway. Go along the grass track on the left, leading to a stile and a waymark. Turn right after this, along Harbour Road (9) back to Rye Harbour.

Points of Interest

Rye Harbour Nature Reserve

The Nature Reserve was established in 1970 and is designed to conserve the plants, animals, birds and waterlife that exist in this lowland area. It is also a Site of Special Scientific Interest and at the entrance to the Car Park at Rye Harbour is an Information Centre, full of details and photographs about the entire Reserve.

Royal Military Canal

At the foot of Winchelsea Hill, a short distance beyond the bridlepath to Camber Castle, lies the Royal Military Canal. The Canal was built between 1804 and 1809 as a defence system across the marshes, which otherwise provided rather too easy access for raids by the French. It begins at the foot of the cliffs at Fairlight and stretches across Romney Marsh to Seabrook in Kent. The Royal Military Canal Path is part of a planned walkway that will eventually run alongside the complete canal. At the moment two sections are open, from Pett to Iden Lock, which is nine miles, and a further five miles between Stutfall Castle and Seabrook.

Camber Castle

Camber Castle was built during the reign of Henry VIII to defend Rye from possible invasion. It had five circular bastions, a central tower and a network of tunnels; work on it was completed in 1543. Unfortunately, its use as a defence lasted a little less than a hundred years, due to the receding coastline and in 1640 it was abandoned. Over a period of time it fell into a state of ruin and was finally closed off for safety reasons in 1967. Considerable repairs have been carried out since then and visits can now be made by arrangement, through the Rye Heritage Centre.

The internal tower at Camber Castle.

Walk 10

BREDE, POWDERMILL RESERVOIR AND BROAK OAK

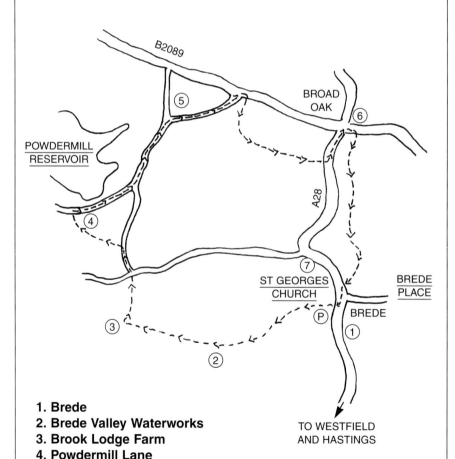

1. Brede
2. Brede Valley Waterworks
3. Brook Lodge Farm
4. Powdermill Lane
5. Goatham Green
6. Broad Oak
7. St. Georges Church

Walk 10

BREDE, POWDERMILL RESERVOIR AND BROAD OAK

Distance	Approx. 5 miles.
Route	Brede - Brede Valley Waterworks - Brook Lodge Farm - Powdermill Lane - Goatham Green - Broad Oak - St. George's Church - Brede.
Maps	O/S Pathfinder 1291 and 1271.
Start/Parking	By St George's Church in Brede, sited on the A28 to Hastings.
Public Transport	Local Rider 300/301, Rye to Brede. Local Rider 400/401, Hastings to Rolvenden.
Conditions	An undulating trail with some of the bridleways being tarmaced.
Refreshments	The Rainbow Trout, Broad Oak. The Red Lion, Brede.

The wide flat landscape of the Brede Levels, its patchwork of fields knitted together with silver flashes of water, lies between a wooded escarpment to the north and some gentle hills to the south. Large flocks of sheep graze amongst the watery meadows; willows line the banks, their leaves turning in the breeze; whilst herons, knee deep in the dykes, wait motionless for a passing fish.

A peaceful scene. Not so, once upon a time, for this area and its inhabitants formed a part of the iron industry, when three hundred years ago, Sussex lay at the heart of industrial England. Hereabouts place names still bear witness to it; such as Forge Stream, Powdermill Bridge, Fryman's Lane and the like.

Brede itself, is an attractive village, with one of the most beautiful rural churches in Sussex. It overlooks the Levels towards Winchelsea and Rye, where the River Brede joins the Tillingham and the Rother before reaching the sea.

The walk starts by the church, then passes through the Brede valley for a mile and a half before penetrating in the exceedingly pretty lanes and woods that surround Powdermill Reservoir. The Rainbow Trout, the first class halfway refreshment stop, is in reality two thirds of the way, at Broad Oak. From here it is only a mile or so, through pleasant countryside, back to Brede.

Interestingly, there are several vineyards in this part of the world. So if there a little time to spare at the end of the day, a visit to the nearest, either the Carr-Taylor Vineyards at Westfield or Sedlescombe Vineyard at Cripp's Corner, could be fun.

St Georges Church, Brede.

Sun across the Brede levels.

Route Directions

Follow the tarmac bridlepath that passes to the south of the church in Brede (1). There is also a 'Southern Water' sign at the entrance. Descend the track passing the Brede Valley Waterworks (2) on the left. Go through the iron gates ahead by a notice saying 'God's Acre Farm'. Keep to the right and after the next iron gate and stile, proceed with the fence to the right, crossing a further stile by a copse. Carry on until reaching a gate adjacent to a large pylon. After this make for Brook Lodge Farm (3) in the foreground, turning right by a converted oast. At the top of the track turn left, then almost immediately right up a road. Go left at a wide entrance to a field, just after a corner. There is a Public Footpath sign at ground level, but like so many, difficult to find. Walk across the first part of the field, then bear right around the perimeter of the second. Although planted when we were there, the farmer had been good enough to leave vague footpath tracks.

Now climb over a stile in the far corner, into woodland. Bear right through the trees and right again at Powdermill Lane (4). From here one can catch a glimpse of Powdermill Reservoir. Turn left at a T-junction and continue up an extremely pretty lane for half a mile, turning right at the next junction. This little area is called Goatham Green (5). Carry on until reaching the main road then go right and instantly right again, along a bridlepath. Once again there is an obscure footpath sign and also a board saying 'Cherry Orchard'. Follow the track until reaching the entrance to Cherry Cottages, on the right, then negotiate the rather overgrown footpath ahead. Cross a stile, a field and another stile. After the next field and stile turn right down a narrow gully, which does become a track, then bear left over a field to a gate behind some corrugated barns. Turn left up the concrete path. Cross the road ahead, bearing left along the high footpath leading into Broad Oak (6).

At the crossroads (the pub will be to the left at this point), turn right and just after the garage, turn right again along a footpath. After a kissing gate, go past some scrappy sheds, climb a stile and continue over the field to a further kissing gate, opening into woodland. Now traverse the stile on the far side of the copse and take the footpath that leads across the field, behind some bungalows , then over another field. Climb a stile. Cross the field and after the gate, keeping the pond and fence to the left, proceed towards St. George's Church (7) (easily seen from here) at Brede. Go over a stile and with the hedge to the left, make for the narrow path that passes between the houses beyond. At the road turn left back into the village.

Points of Interest

St. George's Church, Brede.

The oldest part of this handsome church faces south and dates from the 12th century. Beyond an oak screen, is a keystone with a dog tooth decoration, from the 13th century. The fragments of Flemish glass in the windows over the porch are 14th or 15th century and the east window of the chantry is in Caen stone, erected in the 16th century. The interesting Alms Box is 17th century and the altar is modern. It appears that each era has left a marked impression on the church and the wealth of detail and interest in both the building and its furnishing, make it a compelling place to visit.

The tall and unusual wooden statue of the Madonna was carved by the well known sculptor and writer, Clare Sheridan. The wood used came from the parkland of her home, Brede Place and it was sculpted in memory of her son, Richard, who died at the age of twenty-one. Clare Sheridan died in 1970 and is buried in Brede churchyard.

Brede Place.

About a mile to the east of the village lies Brede Place, a beautiful Tudor Manor and once the home of Sir Goddard Oxenbridge (the family tombs are in the church). This man, who was of unusually large stature, was a gentle giant, but at some time, legend spun an intricate yarn about him. It implies he was a horrendous ogre, who fed on a diet of little children until one day, all the children of the area got together and captured him. They then proceeded to saw him in half with a wooden saw at Groaning Bridge. His ghost supposedly still haunts Brede Place.

Powdermill Reservoir.

The name 'Powdermill' occurs fairly frequently in this part of Sussex, mainly due to the number of mills here that produced gunpowder until the early part of the nineteenth century. The reservoir was flooded about seventy years ago to provide water for Hastings. You will find there are a number of trails that lead into the attractive woods that surrounds it, but only a few are public footpaths, so do check first.

The Wooden Madonna by Clare Sheridan.

Walk 11

NORTHIAM TO BECKLEY

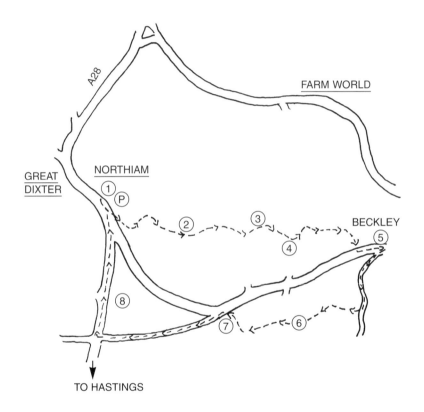

1. Northiam
2. Sussex Border Path
3. Woodgate Farm
4. Rectory Lane
5. Beckley
6. Milldown Wood
7. Clayhill
8. Brickwall Park

Walk 11

NORTHIAM TO BECKLEY

Distance	Approx. 4³/₄ miles.
Route	Northiam - Sussex Border Path - Woodgate Farm - Rectory Lane - Beckley - Milldown Wood - Clayhill - Brickwall Park - Northiam.
Maps	O/S Pathfinder 1271.
Start/Parking	At the Car Park in front of the church in Northiam, on the A28, the Broad Oak to Tenterden road.
Public Transport	Local Rider 348 and 300. 400/401 from Hastings.
Conditions	An easy trail, the only drawback being the last half a mile, which is done along the main road to Northiam. However, there is a wide paved footpath throughout, so it is quite safe.
Refreshments	The Royal Oak, Beckley. The Rose and Crown, Clayhill. The Crown and Thistle or The Six Bells in Northiam.

A gentle undemanding walk through leafy lanes, woods and fields. When we visited, the area was rich in autumn hues, with the bright berries of hips, haws and nightshade dotting the landscape. It is also a walk that offers a spectacular variety of funghi, most of which can probably be eaten, although apart from mushrooms, I have never plucked up enough courage to try any of them. One specie, frequently seen here, is definitely poisonous and should not be tried on any account; nevertheless, it is very beautiful and goes by the name of 'Fly Agaric'. The large scarlet cap, flecked with white scales, makes it easily recognisable.

At Northiam the oaks and chestnuts of Brickwall Park had scattered the surrounding lanes with acorns and conkers, whilst the first fallen leaves of

October dusted the Green. Northiam itself is an attractive village, the timbered houses echoing the Kentish style of building. The fine Hall House of Great Dixter lies on its western edge. By contrast, Beckley is a straggling village that possesses a good pub and a church with early Norman features. The iron industry once flourished hereabouts , as is evident from some of the local place names. A little to the north lies Farm World, a children's farm, an attraction that could keep both the young and the old busy for hours, if it's too wet for walking.

Route Directions

Leave the Car Park in Northiam (1) by the steps in the top left corner. Bear right, down past the church, briefly touch the main road and turn left by a small Green, on to the Sussex Border Path (2); it is signed. Go through an iron gate and keep to the left of the field, passing beyond another iron gate at the bottom and crossing a meadow. Turn left about two-thirds of the way down at a footpath sign and walk straight across the field (unless it is planted, then use the edge) into woodland opposite. Traverse a footbridge and the field ahead. The buildings of Woodgate Farm (3) will be to the left. Cross a footbridge and stile, then almost instantly, another stile on the right. Keep to the left of the field, cross a stile and turn up the track. Go left then right into Rectory Lane (4). Just after a large house, turn left by a wooden fence and gate, which is the entrance to some stables. There is a footpath sign on the other side of the road. After the stables cross a gate, a field then a footbridge and stile on the right. Keep to the left, going over a stile by some trees. Turn right, follow the perimeter of the field until reaching the gate on the far side. Proceed along the bridleway towards some houses, turning left at the road. The Royal Oak at Beckley (5) is on the right a little further on.

From the pub follow the lane that runs along the far side of it. Continue past a bend and up the hill, bearing right across a stile, opposite a farm and farmhouse. Traverse the stile ahead and almost immediately cross another on the right and then a further one, on the other side of a small field. Make for the copse, called Milldown Wood (6) in the foreground and go over the waymarked stile leading into it. Cross a footbridge and proceed to the other side of the woodland, ignoring first, the footpath to the right and then one to the left.

Sunflowers, growing wild.

Queen Elizabeth's I oak tree in Northiam.

After the stile, which leads into a field, stay to the right and cross a further stile into a lane. Turn left, then almost straight away, turn right along a footpath. Traverse a stile, a gateway and the next two fields. Cross the stile ahead, then another on the right, making for a further one on the opposite side of the field. Pass the side of a house and turn left on reaching the road at Clayhill (7). The Rose and Crown will be opposite. Follow the road sign to Staplecross and bear right, along a tarmac lane opposite a timbered cottage. This travels along the edge of the beautiful but private Brickwall Park (8). Proceed until reaching the main road. Turn right and walk along the paved footpath back to Northiam.

Points of Interest

Northiam

An appealing village, lying a mile or so south of the River Rother and having some good examples of beamed and timbered buildings, a couple of pubs, a smattering of shops and plenty of history.

On the delightful village green stands the remains of an oak tree, under which, Queen Elizabeth I picnicked on her way to Rye in 1573. A tiny notice on its massive trunk, held together with chains, tells the full tale. Behind, the splendid spire of St. Mary's soars above the trees; the construction of the church dates mostly from the fifteenth and sixteenth centuries. Just south of the rather sumptuously housed village water pump is the Elizabethan manor of Brickwall, home of the Frewen family, one of whom was made Archbishop of York, after the Restoration of Charles II. Now it is a school and on certain occasions open to the public.

It seems that each time one turns a corner in this village, something else of interest meets the eye; from the massive manor of Dixter, the handsome Church House with a William and Mary frontage or the minute cottage that claims to be the smallest in Sussex.

Great Dixter

An impressive 15th century Hall House on the western side of Northiam. Until the property was purchased in 1910 by Mr. Nathaniel Lloyd, it was actually two separate hall houses, Dixter and Benenden. Both were derelict. Sir Edwin Lutyens, who had been retained by Mr. Llyod, restored both houses and by building an additional wing, made them into one large manor with landscaped gardens. The main hall is enormous, measuring 41 feet by 26 feet, by 31 feet high and the hefty timbers that once supported a Horsham stone roof, have unusual carvings on them. The estate is open to visitors from April to October.

Farm World

Great Knelle Farm at Beckley is a mixed working farm with about 600 acres. Their leaflet stresses they are not a zoo and amongst the animals they keep are cows, ponies, donkeys, pigs, sheep and 'Sussex Specials'. The leaflet also indicates that, with this lot, help at feeding time by anybody wishing to do so, is very welcome. There are various other attractions within the complex including a rabbit village for the children, a farm shop and a restaurant. With all this, it seems a shame it's open only from April to October.

Walk 12

COODEN (BEXHILL) AND NORMAN'S BAY

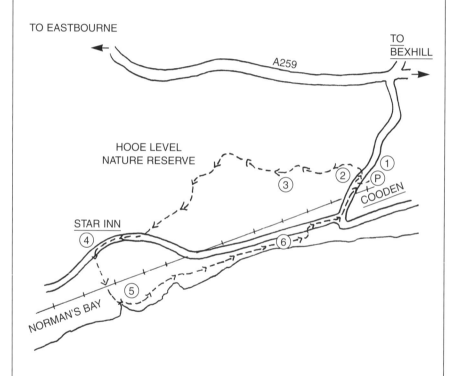

1. Cooden
2. Clavering Walk
3. Cooden Beach Golf Course
4. Star Inn
5. Norman's Bay
6. Beach Huts

Walk 12

COODEN (BEXHILL) AND NORMAN'S BAY

Distance	Approx. 3³/₄ miles.
Route	Cooden - Clavering Walk - Cooden Beach Golf Course - Star Inn - Norman's Bay - Beach Huts - Cooden.
Maps	O/S Pathfinder 1309.
Start/Parking	A Car Park sited at 'The Gorses', opposite Cooden Beach Railway station. About a mile from the A259 at Little Common.
Public Transport	Good bus services from most areas to Bexhill. British Rail to Cooden Beach.
Conditions	An easy coastal walk, but offering little protection in wet or windy weather.
Refreshments	The Star Inn, Norman's Bay. The Sovereign Tavern at the Cooden Resort Hotel, Cooden.

A walk that is unlike any other in this book as the return route travels along the actual beach of the oddly neglected seashore at Norman's Bay. Yet, somehow the air of neglect, coupled with the sound of the waves drawing the shingle, and the seagulls calling across the groynes, give it a unique atmosphere. Houses dotted in a disorderly fashion, rise from windswept, stony gardens. A train rattles along the line. Above the breakwater boats are pulled up, some at crazy angles, some almost derelict, others still in use. Lobster pots, tangled fishing nets, ropes, even rusty anchors, protrude here and there. Flotsam and jetsam, the odd piece warranting closer investigation, in case it turns out to be Norman treasure, recently washed ashore; but no, so instead of finding a fortune, we found driftwood, often fashioned by the sea, collected shells and threw stones for the dog, who was unwilling to get more than his front paws wet from the salty water. Slowly we wandered towards the line of white beach huts and the more sophisticated properties of Cooden Beach.

The first part of the trail meanders around the fringes of the Cooden Beach Golf Course, all a part of the Hooe Level Nature Reserve, then it crosses marshland and meadows to the Star Inn, once the favourite haunt of smugglers. Pause for a moment outside the Star and look inland from east to west. It's easy to see the large natural harbour that had formed by 1066, when these levels were covered by the sea; an ideal place for William the Conqueror and his soldiers. Is that why they call it 'Norman's Bay'?

Route Directions

Turn left from the Car Park opposite the station at Cooden (1), then right along the Cooden Sea road. Go left after Cooden Beach Golf Course and down Clavering Walk (2). Continue to the end of this road and when you can go no further, turn left on to a track. There is a footpath sign but it is almost obliterated by a hedge. Leave the track when it bears left and proceed ahead through a gap in the fence, crossing the golf course, taking care, in case someone is about to play. After the footpath in the scrub opposite, negotiate two more sections of Cooden Beach Golf Course (3), passing a small shed and keeping to the right. There are some fabulous views of the South Downs at this point. Turn right at a wide footpath fringed with rushes and streams, away from the course. Cross a footbridge, turn left and almost immediately, cross another footbridge and stile. Follow the stream on the left to a further footbridge after which, head for the far right hand corner of the next field. Pass through the gateway and with the fence to the right, make for the stile beyond. Now bear right and follow the road for a short distance until reaching the Star Inn (4).

Soon after the pub, climb the stile on the left and go along the river bank to a small gate. Cross the wooden track spanning the railway line and after a second gate, turn left then right and proceed over the footpath that culminates at Norman's Bay (5). Having reached the shingled beach, turn left, keeping to the top end of the sea shore above the groynes (no need to worry about the tide). From here there is an excellent vista of the entire bay

Flotsam and Jetsam.

from Bexhill to Beachy Head.

Continue straight ahead, past various boats and buildings, including a shed that sells fresh fish. After the line of immaculately painted beach huts (6), join the road on the far side and walk along the pavement in front of some houses, turning left at the Cooden Resort Hotel at Cooden. Pass under the railway bridge and back to the Car Park.

Points of Interest

Cooden

Cooden has really become a 'suburb' of Bexhill, but it has developed in a very pleasant fashion with large attractive properties. The beach, which can be sandy at low tide, is excellent for swimming.

The Star Inn

This popular fifteenth century inn at Norman's Bay, was originally built as a sluice keepers cottage when Pevensey Marsh was drained. It became an inn around 1550 and reports indicate it was the last stronghold of smuggling in Sussex.

Bexhill

Bexhill has an extensive and attractive seafront with the striking De La Warr Pavilion in a central position. This was opened in 1935 and its Art Deco style also suggests a strong continental influence. It can be visited throughout the year and a wide range of entertainments and events are held there. The old part of Bexhill, just north of the pavilion and reached by following the sea road, still retains its rural character with quaint houses and shops. Nearby, in Manor Gardens, is the Bexhill Costume and Social History Museum.

By the beach huts at Cooden.

POINTS TO REMEMBER

1) Keep to public Rights of Way.

2) Fasten all gates.

3) Keep dogs under control.

4) Do not leave litter around.

5) Do not disturb cattle, sheep or other animals.

6) Do not pick wild flowers.

7) Leave the countryside as you find it so others can enjoy it too.

Please Note

Very occasionally suggested routes or diversions may not automatically imply a right of way. In order to satisfy themselves they are not trespassing, walkers should seek permission when in doubt.

'From Woods to Fields'.

TRANSPORT AND INFORMATION

British Rail: Train times and fares - Tel (01273) 206755

Bus Services: Bus Helpline - Tel (01273) 478007

Tourist Information Centres

Battle	88, High Street.	Tel (01424) 773721
Bexhill	De La Warr Pavilion	Tel (01424) 212023
Boship	Lower Dicker	Tel (01323) 442667
Hastings	4, Robertson Terrace.	Tel (01424) 781111
Pevensey	Castle Cottage.	Tel (01323) 761444
Rye	Heritage Centre, Strand Quay	Tel (01797) 226696